I DON'T FETCH

AND OTHER POEMS FOR CAT LOVERS

I DON'T FETCH

AND OTHER POEMS FOR CAT LOVERS

By Steve Dambrosio

Illustrations by
Shilpa R. Badadare

Lyrical Cat Publishing

ISBN: 978-0-9969094-0-2

To Chris, who taught me to love cats, and to agree wholeheartedly that one cat per household is never enough! And of course to our wonderful cats, here with us or gone hunting in the fertile hereafter, whom I have served faithfully for many happy years. In exchange for my obedience and devotion they have provided a wealth of antics about which I may wax poetically. Thank you sincerely Bubba, Sissy, Seven, and Diva.

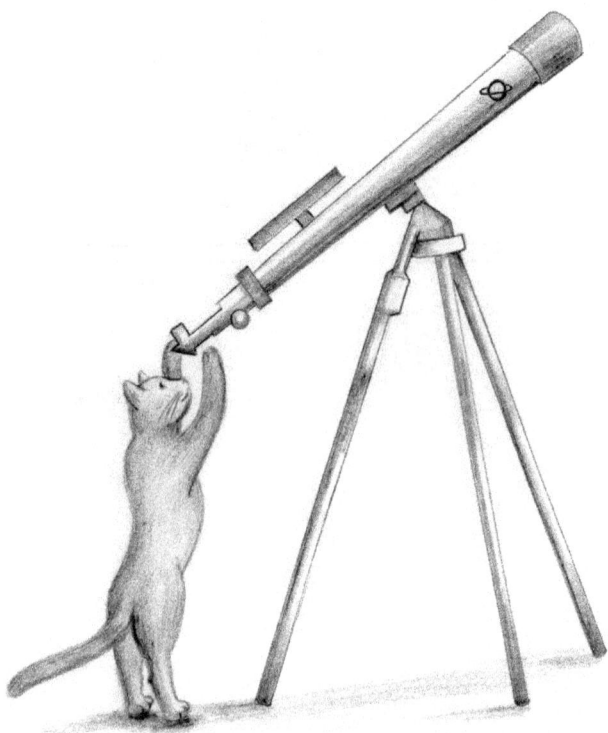

The Cosmic Perspective

THE SIX TRILLIONTH DAY

On the Six Trillionth Day
    (give or take a few billion years . . .)
The Great Creator of all things
    looked down upon her handiwork
And saw that it was good . . .
    but not good enough!

"I have yet to make my masterpiece," she declared.

"A creature of nobility,
With natural ability
To leap beyond its earthly tether
And touch down lightly as a feather.
A creature fast and sleek and strong
(but not too short and not too long)
Whose coat shines in a fashion show
Of Midnight Black to Calico.
With sharpened tooth and claw to fight
And glowing eyes that see at night.
With prickly whiskers on its face
To navigate a narrow place.
A voice to croon a sweet refrain
Or screech and howl a hurricane!
With magical powers beyond all that—
Can pull a rabbit from a hat."

And so She sat,
    And thought,
      And sat,
        And in Her image—
          She made the Cat!

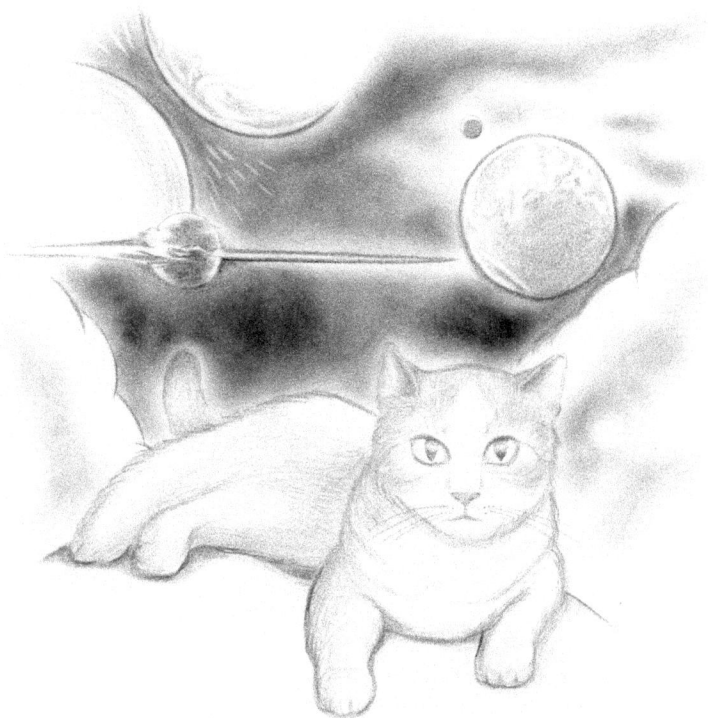

The Human Perspective

HAVE YOU SEEN BLINKY?

Have you seen Blinky, my invisible cat?
I've looked everywhere—
    Don't know where he's at.
Under the table? High up on a shelf?
Curled up in a nook just to be by himself?
I've looked in the bedroom, gave the bed sheets a tug,
Examined the bathroom and searched in the tub.
I even checked under the rug!
I looked in some places you normally wouldn't,
And other strange places a sane person shouldn't,
But in all of these cases—
    I just couldn't!
Find Blinky, my invisible cat.

ICK!

I can't believe my cat turned down
His can of Seafood Mix.
It's got to taste far better than
Some places that he licks!

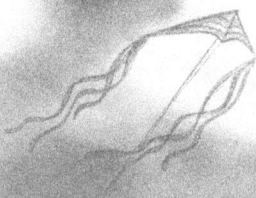

THE ELEVENTH DIMENSION

Did I ever mention
The eleventh dimension?
A place where no human may tread.
It's a place you can slide
In and out of your hide
Or ooze through the floor
To the dimension next door
Or snooze on a cloud
And . . . did I ever mention?
Only cats are allowed.

It's where a cat goes
When he's right under your nose
Then suddenly he simply is not!
You holler "KITTY KITTY"
Till you wake the whole CITY CITY!
And search low and high
Then give up with a sigh.
But he's in the same place—
Just not taking up space.
Not in our world, that is
And, Gee-Whiz!
Did I ever mention? . . .
How I hate the eleventh dimension!

SAY IT IN "CAT"

I think I'll give my back a pat.
I've learned the language of my cat!
A "meow" for a human greeting,
A "yeeeeooow" to call a cat meeting,
A "chatter" when a bird is near,
(and stony silence when in fear)
A "hiss" to start a boxing match,
A "purrrr" to thank me for a scratch,
A "grrrrr" to put a foe in line,

But woe is me

She thinks it fine

To never learn a word of mine!

JAZZ CATS AND THE FIDDLE

Felix plays the fiddle but he can't play all alone.
Let's get Thomas Little on the slide trombone.
And on the coolest ax
We have Sissy on the sax.
And on the jazzy trumpet
Bring in Jasper from Nantucket.

Now we need a beat—
A funky-monkey beat.
To get your noggin bobbin' with the tappin' in your feet.
And who of all us cats is best to beat the tom-tom drums?
A hi-hat cat to set the groove all night
    till morning comes?
Look! Here comes Tabby Rose!
Spinning drumsticks with her toes!
So now we have a drummer . . .
    But now we need a strummer.
Oh, Bo can play the banjo!
And of course we've got to make some space
    For Maisie on the electric bass.

Now, with the band complete
We can't forget the part for me—
A most important part indeed
I'm sure you will agree.

And though I cannot play a toot
You'll never find me napping,
For I shall be the audience
 And so provide the clapping!

HAIR!

Hair!

There is hair.

You say where? Everywhere!

Coating the sofa and there on the chair.

My poor cat is shedding her hair, and I swear—

My slacks are as fuzzy as Wuzzy was bare.

Where,

Oh dear, where—

Does she get all that hair?

It's took to the wind and it's clogging the air.

My nose is all stuffed and I'm feeling despair.

'Cause it's even invaded my clean underwear!

Fair?

It's not fair

That my cat's a longhair.

And I wasn't aware that she'd shed with such flair.

And I find it so hopeless (and I haven't a prayer),

I've asked her to stop but she just doesn't care.

But look at that sweetheart!

See her there? By the stair.

I suppose for all that a few hairs I can bear.

And what? . . .

What is her name you ask?

It's Claire.

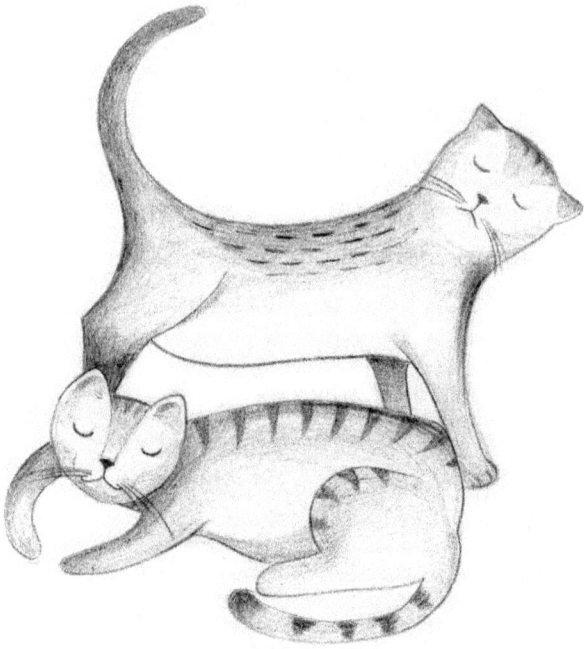

MY LAZY CATS

My cats are lazy ones for sure.
They haven't got the strength to purr.
I watch them lying still for hours.
Get up cats and smell the flowers!
Catching mice would be a cinch
If only you would budge one inch!

In the morning when I rise
They hardly open up their eyes,
And when I'm putting on my socks
They're sleeping soundly in their box,
And when I'm putting on my shoes
They're starting on a second snooze,
And when I'm straightening up my tie
They're giving it just one more try,
And when I'm putting on my jacket
They sleep right through the loudest racket,
And when I'm out and slam the door
They just nap a little more
    and more
       and more
          and more.
             What a bore!
Snore . . . zzzzzzz

TOMMY B. GOOD

I know a cat . . .
    named Tommy B. Good.
The sneakiest, slinkiest cat in the hood.
The kind that would scratch you
    when you're least suspecting
With one of the silent attacks he's perfecting.

He doesn't like poodles or penguins or pigeons,
Dowdy old dowagers or crotchety curmudgeons.
Doesn't like bikes or convertible cars,
Not even Jupiter, Saturn or Mars.
He doesn't like babies or *anything* soft,
Boats on the water or kites flown aloft,
Brown paper packages tied up with strings,
Surely not any of *my* favorite things.
Doesn't like apples or pickles or nickels,
Dollars or quarters or tootsie popsicles.
Winters or summers or autumns or springs,
Bright blooming flowers or butterfly wings.

How can a fine cat like that be so sour,
Sitting and sulking for hour after hour?
Now, here's an idea that perhaps I should mention!
Maybe he needs just a bit more attention.

Maybe a brush or a stroke on his fur
Would turn a mean growl on the prowl to a *purrrrrrr*.
And then he might like all the things that he should,
That sneakiest, slinkiest Tommy B. Good.

SWEET SOUNDS

A rush of wind through waves of grain.
The hush of snowflakes falling.
Swirling leaves in garden's lane—
The sound of autumn calling.
A mother's hush as baby cries.
The cooing of a dove.
Dramatic adolescent sighs—
And whispered words of love.
The patter of a falling rain
To start the day anew.
The solace of a song's refrain.
A promise to be true.
A tune to soothe the savage breast.
A voice that's reassuring.
And last,
    but oh, by far the best—
A tiny kitten purring.

GET DOWN

Get down!
The counter is off limits!
Don't lie on the bed!
Get off of the table!
Don't jump on the desk!
Come down off the bookshelf!
Stay out of the sink!
Away from the pillow!
Now, follow the rules!
Your honor is bound
. . . but . . .
Feel free to ignore them when I'm not around.

HOOK THE CURLY-Q CAT

Hook the curly-Q cat
He's curly but not only that!
His tail is a corkscrew, his whiskers sublime.
They twist and they twirl like your tongue on this rhyme.
He's truly an oddball yet simply divine.
He's Hook the curly-Q cat.

Hook the fuzzy feline
How often I wish he were mine!
He's quite a sensation, but I must forewarn:
He looks like a sheep that forgot to be shorn.
His pedigree's lost but I'm sure he's well-born.
He's Hook the fuzzy feline.

So many furballs, they're piled on the floor.
After you comb him he's crying for more.
How can a cat with lines so broken
Fly straight and true through a door left open?

Hook the curly-Q cat
No finer a cat was begat!
He'll leave in the morning and stay out all night,
Appear out of nowhere to give you a fright,
You may hear him singing by dawn's early light.

He's Hook the curly-Q cat.

That's *that!*

FORGIVENESS

My cat destroyed my favorite chair
But I forgave her.
It's only fair.
Then she chewed my favorite shoe
And I forgave again.
It's true.
The cat-box was an awful mess—
Shall I forgive again?
I guess.
She coughed a soggy ball of fur
And I forgave again.
For sure.
She caught a tiny field mouse
And let it loose right in the house!
Would I forgive that naughty deed?
Yes I did. I did indeed.
I could go on
and on
and on
But you'd get bored real soon,
Because the times that I forgave
Would stretch clear to the moon.

PUSSIN' ON THE RITZ

Tom Cat Fritz
Is pussin' on the Ritz—
Top cat, white tie and tail.
A cat to write home about.
A cat to watch roam about town.
Prowlin' with his lady-cat,
His feline-fancy lady-cat,
Bejeweled
    Befurred
        Besparkling in her gown.
They trip the light fantastic
And paint the city red.
They prance the dance gymnastic
Till there's spinning in his head.
Then she, in misty reverie
Begins a feline song.
A sweet and haunting melody
To make his heart grow fond.
But soon the cool moon finds its journey's end
As morning calls.
And with one kiss they part.
But not before he falls—
    In love.
Dove wings flutter as she flees into the night.

Was it just a dream?
A fancy of my wits?
Only questions greet the dawn from
     Tom Cat Fritz.

SHYAM THE MAGNIFI-CAT

Shyam is a cat.
He's a magical cat.
And the whole world spins on his tail.
He's black as night
And he'll scratch and bite
If you don't say his name just right!

(Drum roll please! . . .)

SHYAM the magnifi-cat
SHYAM the terrifi-cat
SHYAM the magnanimal, wonderful animal.
Strong as a lion
When he's barely tryin'
All tremble wherever he goes.
He's royalty head to his toes!

(Fanfare please! . . .)

When he was just a young lad
And fit in the palm of your hand,
His castle was merely a brown paper box,
His bed was a t-shirt,
His throne a bundle of socks.

Now he keeps a watchful eye
From a scratching post that's ten feet high,
And he'll scratch his claws so carelessly
On any fine fabric he doth see!

Oh!—

SHYAM the invincible
SHYAM the unflinchable
SHYAM the divine and a very fine feline.
He's quicker than lightning.
I tell you that's fright'ning.
He'll disappear into thin air
And do it with élan and flair!

(Fanfare please! . . .)

What a hero! Fancy that!
A tried and true Magnifi-cat.
He'll go down by his decree
As the greatest cat in history.

One more word before I go—
He's the truest friend I know.
And when he's sleeping all is calm.
Magnifi-cat Shyam.

ATTACK!

Watch out!
A lick attack!
Here it comes!
An itch attack!
Oh my!
A cuddle attack!
My cat's . . .
An ATTACK CAT!

I LOVE CATS

I love cats.
Of course I do!
    Don't you?
Young cats and old cats.
Shy cats and bold cats.
Fat cats and skinny cats.
Gigantic cats and mini cats.
Cats with stripes and cats with spots.
Cats so round they're shaped like pots.
The cat down the street.
The cat that's at your feet.
The cat you've never seen before
    but soon you're gonna meet.
Cats as fierce as tigers,
Or stealthy like the leopard.
Cats whose coats are black or white
    or lightly salt and peppered.
Cats that meow a lovely song
And ask you please to sing along,
Or cats that suffer purring spells
    that measure sixty decibels!
Cats out hunting in the woods
Or prowling city neighborhoods.
Cats stuck high up in a tree
Or cozy curled on top of me.

So many cats to love . . . it's true!

But I love them all.

   Don't you?

The Feline Perspective

MY BASKET

I love this basket of mine.
It's so warm and cozy.
I wouldn't dare mosey or wander too far.
I haven't a clue where the other cats are.
I don't care what time it is—got no use for clocks.
I won't even get up to pee in my box.
I think I'll just snooze till then end of all time
And dream lovely dreams in this basket of mine.

LITTLE FISHIES

I love the little fishies,
Swimming in their bowl,
Swimming to and fro.
And they don't have a hunch
That swimming in a bunch
Makes me want to reach inside
And scoop them up for lunch!

THE FINICKY EATER

I don't like Brand X.
I don't like Brand Y.
I don't like Brand Z either.
I suppose I'm a finicky eater.

I don't eat chicken.
I don't eat tuna.
I don't like the stink of it.
And leftovers? Don't even think of it!

If only they'd put all the food that I like in a can
It would fly off the shelf.
But *sigh* . . . till they do
I'll just muddle through
And go out and catch it myself!

DRIP

Drip
Drip
Drip
    Lick
    Lick
    Lick
Drip
Drip
Drip
    Lick
    Lick
    Lick

Forever may my faucet drip!
Leave it on and let it spill.
Drink until I've had my fill.
    And the best part is? . . .
I don't pay the water bill.

PLEASE, PLEASE

If only I could get outside
And run across the grass.
It hurts my nose to press it up
So hard against this glass!
Every time a bird goes by
My teeth begin to chatter.
With one less bird up in the sky
Do ya think it'd really matter?
You see, I was born a hunter
And I long to have my prey.
Won't you let me out to chase some mice
For just one day?
I'd frolic in the garden
And I'd climb up every tree.
I'd bat around the butterflies
And bite a honey bee.
I'd shadow box the daisies
And I'd stalk a salamander,
Or maybe find a shady spot
Beneath the oleander.
I'd sit and watch the world go by
And sniff what's on the breeze.
Is that so much to ask of you?
Oh please, oh please, oh please!
Can't you see my pain and sorrow?

Oh . . .

Looks like rain . . .

I think I'll go outside tomorrow!

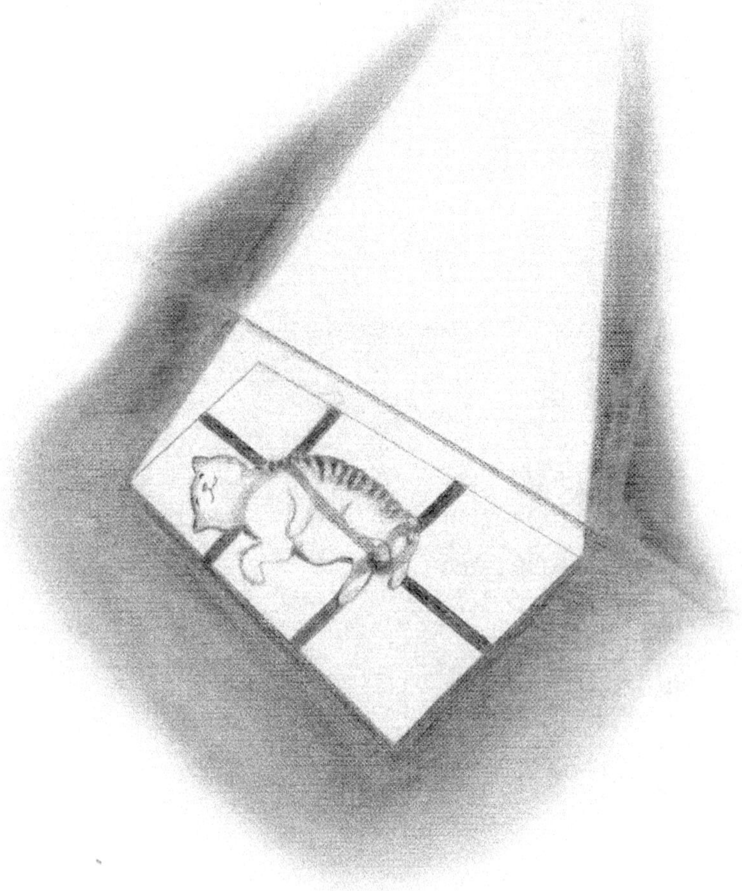

MY PATCH OF LIGHT

My Patch of Light,
I love you so.
I'll follow you wherever you go.

Across the landing,
Down
    the
       stairs,
Over the rug,
Up on the chair.

Your rays are warm and feel so nice.
Twice as nice as chasing mice!
I'll catch a nap or two with you
Until you move . . . and I must too!
And when you shrink so very small
Until there's nothing there at all,
I will not weep, my sunny friend,
For never shall our union end.
I'll wait until we meet again.

When all is good
   And all is right,
      Beneath my sunny
         Patch of Light.

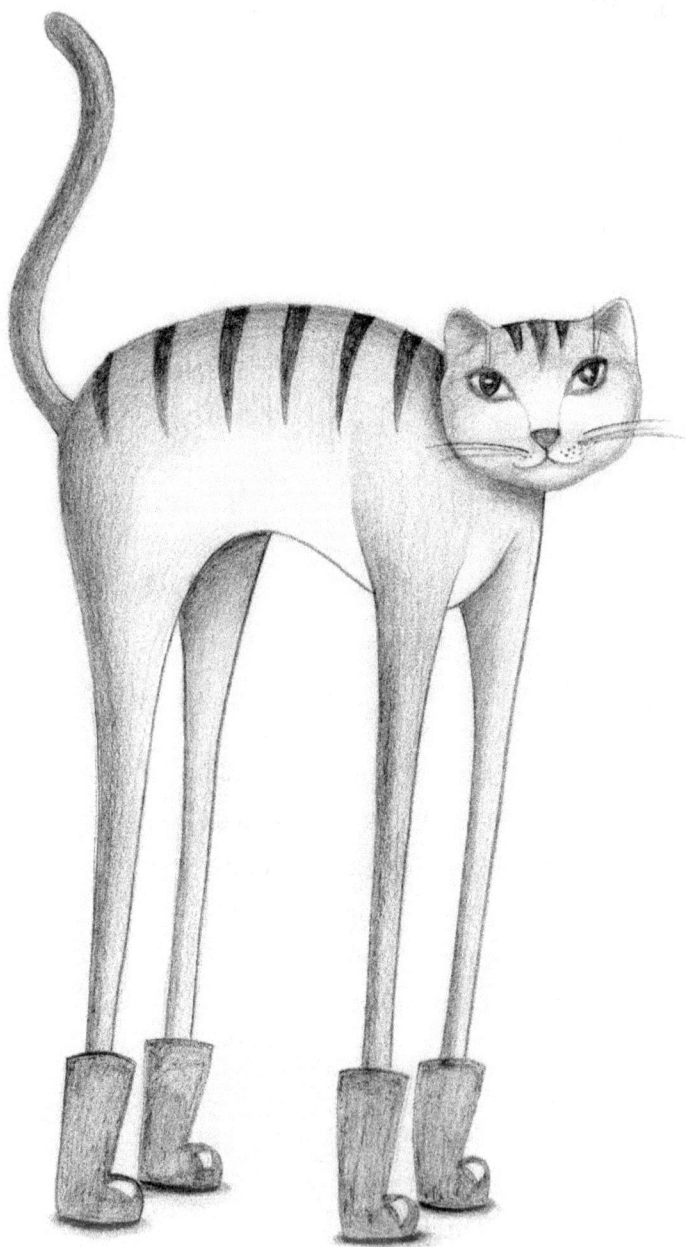

NEVER FEAR

Never fear
My dear.

You can drop me head first.

You can drop me tail first.

You can drop me nose first.

You can drop me seat first.

But never fear
My dear.

I'll always land feet first.

UP, UP, AND AWAY!

The chair is nowhere high enough.
The table's far too low.
The bookshelf's just a stepping stone
To where I want to go.

Even on the rooftop
Or in the highest tree,
I don't believe the altitude
Is high enough for me.

I long to scale the highest peak
Above the clouds and free,
To scan the blue horizon
From sea to shining sea.

Then I'll rear and shake my tail
And leap clear to the Moon,
Looking back upon my world,
The size of a balloon.

Or higher still, if I may dream,
To kiss the twinkling stars,
Or sniff for creatures great or small
On Jupiter or Mars.

Fearlessly I fling myself
Into the swirling void.
Unbounded by the universe
I'm suddenly annoyed!

Alas, my dreams are all for naught.
My little head is reeling.
Because I cannot break beyond
This hard, unyielding ceiling!

MY RELATIONS

My aunt is a tiger.
My uncle's a lion.
My cousin's a leopard with spots.
But I'm just a house cat,
A chase-after-mouse cat,
And covered with white polka-dots!

AAAHH, CHRISTMAS TREE

Here beneath my Christmas Tree,
As happy as a cat can be,
I hide between the silver wraps
And take one hundred kitty naps.
But when I wake what do I see?
Low hanging bobbles just for me!
I paw one gently, then some more,
Until it tumbles to the floor.
Pretending it's a fuzzy mouse
I chase it clear across the house,
Until it hides where I can't get it . . .
I try a while then soon forget it.
It's not a thing to make me glum . . .
There's plenty more where it came from!
But soon I tire of chasing balls
Or other things that deck the halls,
And come back to my secret place
Where I resume a slower pace.
And slower still until I doze,
All curled up to warm my nose,
As happy as a cat can be,
Here beneath my Christmas Tree.

I CAN FIT

You'd think this lovely cardboard box
Is rather small for me,
But I can fit quite easily.
Just stick around . . . you'll see.
But first I've got to meditate,
Because to fit it all
I'll need great mental discipline
To *will* my body small.
Just like the Yogi Master,
I'll shift my limbs about,
And scrunch them very close until
I'm almost inside out.
My head is where my tail should be.
My tail is at my head.
I'm sucking in my rib cage.
(Wish I wasn't so well-fed!)
Compressed into a rectangle
I knew I would prevail.
But although it's rather cozy here
I'm gasping to inhale!
I've got an itch behind my ear,
A cramp in my back leg.
Will someone get me out of here?
It's embarrassing to beg!

Although my box is straining hard
And bursting at the seams,
The thought of breaking free is quite
Beyond my wildest dreams!
Fool am I to think I'd fit
In such a tiny matchbox.
I suppose all hope is lost—
I've turned into a CAT BOX!

I DON'T FETCH

I don't fetch.
I never do tricks.
I haven't a yearning to chase after sticks.
I won't wear a leash
So don't take me for walks.
I'd rather be snoozing all day in my box.
I won't bring the paper
To drop at your feet.
I'll only come running when it's time to eat.
But if I don't like it
I'll turn up my nose.
And if *you* don't like it, well, that's just how it goes!
So if you want someone
To drool at your feet,
And go crazy gaga each time that we meet,
And call you my Master
And do your sweet bidding,
It's time to get real . . . You've got to be kidding!
Go get a *DOG*
Or forget all of *that.*
You must love me simply for being a CAT!

www.ingramcontent.com/pod-product-compliance
Lightning Source LLC
Chambersburg PA
CBHW020605030426
42337CB00013B/1230